Profile of the Southern Moguls

Plate 1: K class locomotives, Nos. 32342 and 32348, await their next turns of duty on Norwood Shed on 11th July 1958.

R. C. Riley

Plate 2: The 10.03 Eastleigh to Fratton freight passes Botley behind N class locomotive No. 31852 on 26th May 1952. The line bearing away to the right under the bridge is the Bishop's Waltham branch, where the passenger service ceased in January 1933. The line closed to all traffic in April 1962.

L. Elsey

PROFILE OF
THE SOUTHERN MOGULS

Les Elsey

Oxford Publishing Company

Plate 3:   A Ramsgate to Victoria train, with N1 class No. 31878 climbing the 1 in 100 incline of Sole Street Bank in rousing style on 18th June 1955.

Stanley Creer

Copyright © 1986 Oxford Publishing Co.

ISBN 0-86093-314-8

Typesetting by:
Aquarius Typesetting Services, New Milton, Hants.

Printed in Great Britain by:
Biddles Ltd., Guildford, Surrey.

Published by:
Oxford Publishing Co.
Link House
West Street
POOLE, Dorset

ACKNOWLEDGEMENTS

My thanks go to all who have contributed photographs and information for this album, and also the *Railway Magazine* and *Institute of Mechanical Engineers* for permission to reproduce the line drawings. Sincere thanks go, to my wife, Daphne, for her help and encouragement to complete this project.

INTRODUCTION

The Mogul family made a significant every day contribution to Southern England's steam operation for the best part of half a century.

The LBSCR produced the K class in 1913, to the designs of L. B. Billinton at Brighton Works, for working goods traffic as, up to that time, double-heading in suburban areas had been avoided. The class was also used to work passenger trains at busy periods when required, which it ultimately carried out very well. At the time of the Grouping in 1923, seventeen locomotives had been completed.

Meanwhile, R. E. L. Maunsell had become CME for the SECR, in the same year designing the N class goods engine with 5ft. 6in. wheels and a passenger 2-6-4T using the same basic parts, but having 6ft. wheels. However, through heavy repair commitments caused by World War I, the two prototypes did not enter traffic until 1917. The N class was probably the first British locomotive to have a combination of high superheat and long travel valves and there was a GWR influence in the use of a taper boiler top feed and Belpaire firebox. By using outside Walschaerts valve gear, this made preparation of a 2-cylinder engine much easier, there being no need to go over a pit to oil the motion. After a period of testing and development, fifteen N class locomotives were built in SECR days.

When the Southern Railway was formed, Maunsell became the CME for that group of railways and, in 1924, trials were carried out on the Western Section with the LBSCR K class and the SECR N class hauling a heavy loaded goods train, to decide which design would be most suitable for future construction in the coming years. The Class K's performance was disappointing whilst the N class was adequate, although as mixed traffic locomotives there was little to choose between them. With its cheaper maintenance and better showing, the N class was chosen as the basis for the future as a secondary passenger locomotive, culminating in the U and U1 classes in 1931, plus the opportunity of interchangeability of parts and boilers between the classes.

The ex-SECR Moguls were nicknamed 'Woolworths' by the enginemen, and the U class were well liked by the crews. They rarely strayed from the Western Section whereas the N class, in particular, gave sterling service on the West Country and the Kent Coast lines, especially on summer Saturdays in the 1950s.

During the closing stages of steam on the Southern Region of British Railways there were 174 Moguls, including 17 of the Brighton design, which no doubt could have carried on for a few more years if electrification had not arrived over the greater part of the system.

Les Elsey
Bishopstoke
Hants
1985

Plate 4: U class Mogul No. 31808, with a Portsmouth Harbour to Weymouth excursion, passing through the New Forest near Beaulieu Road, on 8th July 1956.

L. Elsey

CONTENTS

K Class

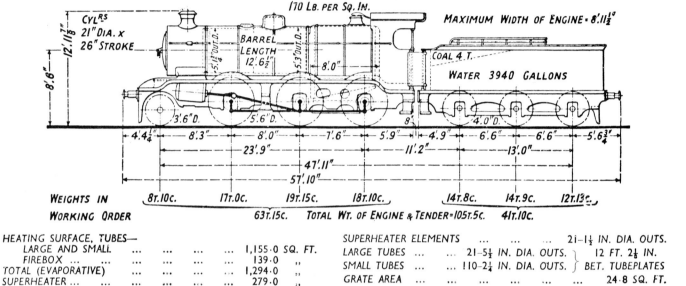

Recent change not shown on drawing : boiler pressure increased to 180 lb. per sq. in.

Figure 1: A drawing of a K class locomotive, showing the engine as running with modified cab and boiler fittings in Southern Railway days.

Summary of the LBSC K class Locomotives

Loco. No.	SR No.	Date Built	Builder	Withdrawn
337	2337	9/13	Brighton	12/62
338	2338	12/13	Brighton	12/62
339	2339	3/14	Brighton	11/62
340	2340	6/14	Brighton	12/62
341	2341	11/14	Brighton	12/62
342	2342	10/16	Brighton	12/62
343	2343	11/16	Brighton	12/62
344	2344	12/16	Brighton	11/62
345	2345	12/16	Brighton	12/62
346	2346	12/16	Brighton	11/62
347	2347	12/20	Brighton	12/62
348	2348	12/20	Brighton	11/62
349	2349	12/20	Brighton	11/62
350	2350	12/20	Brighton	11/62
351	2351	1/21	Brighton	11/62
352	2352	2/21	Brighton	11/62
353	2353	3/21	Brighton	12/62

The K class, designed by L. B. Billinton in 1913, was built to eliminate double-heading of the rebuilt C2X class 0-6-0s on heavy freight duties in the London area, where it was customary to pilot these heavy trains over part of the journey to ensure that the acceleration from sidings and signal stops were such that delays to the suburban services were minimal.

They were simple basic superheated locomotives with two outside cylinders, inside Stephenson's valve gear and 5ft. 6in. driving wheels. They were left-hand drive with a screw reverser and a Weir feed pump for the boiler, although in BR days, by 1953, all were removed to be replaced by cold water injectors. After Nos. 337 and 338 appeared, there were complaints of excessive fire throwing when pulling hard, or unsteady riding above 35m.p.h.

Modifications were made to the smokebox layout and pony truck side control, fitting a 5in. longer smokebox to suit the revised smokebox layout. From then on, all the locomotives were built to the same standard. Various modifications were tried out but, by the end of their life, they proved that although they were mixed traffic engines, they were equally at home working express trains when called upon to do so.

Withdrawal came in late 1962, when they were stored in Hove goods yard, and the majority of the class were towed to Eastleigh Works for scrapping. The exceptions were No. 32347, which was cut up at Stewarts Lane, and Nos. 32337/40/43 which were scrapped at King's of Norwich in March 1964. None were preserved.

Plate 5: No. 337, photographed by the official photographer in 1913, shortly after construction at Brighton Works. It is painted in dove grey, lined out in black and white with white lettering, and with numerals shaded black. This livery was carried until February 1914 when the locomotive was painted plain black.

W. M. J. Jackson Collection

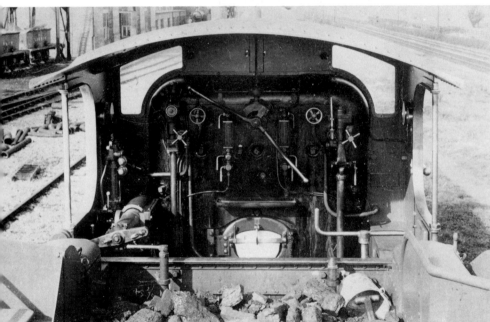

Plate 6: A cab view of No. 337, photographed at Eastbourne in September 1913.

M. G. Joly Collection

Plate 7: No. 350 backs on to the turntable at New Cross Gate in 1921. This locomotive is painted in the normal LBSC goods livery of plain black with yellow numerals and lettering. The top feed is housed in the second dome, to raise the clacks and permit a deeper distributing tray to prevent matter suspended in the water to enter the boiler.

Author's Collection

Plate 8: South of Coulsdon, No. 339 tackles the 1 in 165 climb to Quarry Tunnel with a 'down' Brighton excursion in 1923. This was the type of work that these locomotives could handle quite well when busy periods occurred throughout the summer.

Lens of Sutton

Plate 9: In the first year of service, No. 337 is pictured on a Brighton-bound goods train leaving Littlehampton.

M. J. Joly Collection

Plate 10: No. 347 heads an 'up' goods from Brighton towards Coulsdon in 1923. Nos. 347 and 349 were the first K class locomotives to have Ross 'pop' safety-valves instead of the usual Ramsbottom type, as built.
Author's Collection

Plate 11: No. 342 at New Cross Shed on 14th July 1927. This locomotive has the earlier type of top feed, which consisted of two clacks mounted on a manhole cover on the boiler top. It was running in a mixture of Southern and LBSC liveries, having been painted in LBSC passenger umber livery, with lettering on the tender and numerals on the buffer beam, and carried Southern cast oval cab numberplates.
H. C. Casserley/E. W. Fry Collection

Plate 12: In Southern livery outside Brighton Shed, in April 1926, is No. B343. The Weir feed pump fitted to all the class when built is seen on the left-hand running plate.
Author's Collection

EXPERIMENTS

Plate 13: On No. 351, the smokebox was lengthened to take a Lewis draft appliance, the standard chimney being replaced by an elliptical stove pipe in April 1921. This apparatus was the invention of D. M. Lewis, an American engineer, and was, in effect, a variable blastpipe, automatically controlled by the passage of exhaust steam. At this time No. 351 was painted red oxide with white numerals and no lettering. After a number of trials, the appliance had very little effect on the coal consumption. Nevertheless, the equipment remained in use until January 1927, when it was removed.

E. W. Fry Collection

Plate 14: No. B351 restored to normal although still retaining the extended smokebox but fitted with a standard chimney to give an impression of immense power. It is painted in the green Southern Railway livery and is seen at Brighton in 1927.

E. W. Fry Collection

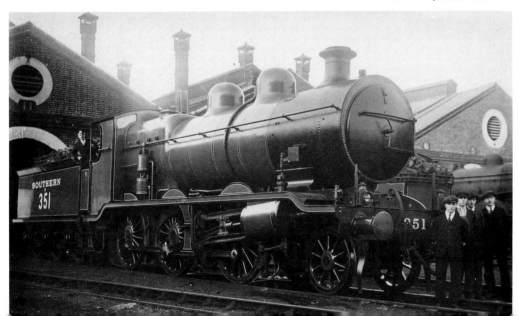

Plate 15: In early SR days, and with the prefix B to denote a former LBSC engine, No. B345 passes Honor Oak Park with an evening commuter train from London Bridge, formed of stock commonly known in those days on that railway as 'Balloons'.

Lens of Sutton

Plate 16: In Southern days, No. B343 passing Lewes with a Brighton-bound freight in the early 1930s. This locomotive is similar to No. B338 (*see Plate 17*) having only the cab modified to the composite loading gauge.

Lens of Sutton

Plate 17: No. B338 prepares to leave East Croydon in 1930, and is bound for Reading, via Redhill, composed of LSWR rolling stock. This locomotive has the cab altered to the composite gauge, but the chimney and domes are still outside the loading gauge to work over the Eastern and Western sections.

Author's Collection

Plate 18: No. 2339, ex-works, photographed at Eastleigh on 16th August 1936, after being modified to conform to the composite loading gauge (i.e. a new cab top, resited whistle, cut down chimney and dome). Other changes were carried out to all members of the class in the 1930s which included backing of the tender coal rails, abandoning of the top feed, fitting of Ross 'pop' safety-valves instead of the Ramsbottom pattern, and Maunsell superheaters replacing the Robinson pattern.

Author's Collection

Plate 19: No. 2342, shown here on Brighton Shed, was the first coal burner, apart from the streamlined classes, to be equipped with electric lighting, and also the first Southern Railway engine to be fitted with the CAV system. The generator is fitted on a bracket on the right-hand cab front to the rear of the Westinghouse pump. The fittings were removed in January 1951.

W. M. J. Jackson

Plate 20: No. 32349, in early BR days, at Eastleigh on 4th July 1952, in plain black with British Railways lettering and numerals, complete with smokebox numberplate and shed plate.

L. Elsey

Plate 21: Standing at Eastleigh on 12th January 1952 is No. 32347, ex-works, in lined black livery, with the first BR small emblem on the tender which was first introduced in 1948. The position of the cab numerals varied between different works.

L. Elsey

CENTRAL SECTION

Plate 22: A heavy ballast train, double-headed by Nos. 32353 and 32352, pulls away from Rowfant, on the Three Bridges to East Grinstead line, in the mid-1950s.

Lens of Sutton

Plate 23: The driver is adjusting his reverser on No. 32340 as he accelerates down the 1 in 122 incline away from West Hoathly with a Brighton to London Bridge train on 21st May 1955.

R. C. Riley

Plate 24: On 20th June 1957, No. 32348 emerges into the early morning sunshine from Cliftonville Tunnel, on the Hove to Preston Park spur line, with empty stock from Hove Sidings to Brighton (Lovers' Walk) carriage washer. The engine, on arrival at Preston Park, backs the train through the washer into Brighton Station. The stock then forms the Brighton to Plymouth through train, via the coast line.

J. W. Kent

Plate 25: A Hastings to Manchester (SO) through train passes Kensington north signal box, on the West London line, on 22nd August 1959, headed by No. 32342. Locomotive changing will be carried out at Willesden, where a London Midland Region locomotive will take over.

R. C. Riley

Plate 26: In 1950, faced with a shortage of rolling stock, the SR's South Western Division borrowed several sets of air-braked Eastern Region suburban stock of Great Eastern origin for specials to the Farnborough Air Show. To work these trains were several classes of ex-LBSCR locomotives, fitted with dual brakes (Atlantics, Class B4X 4-4-0s, and K classes). No. 32348 approaches Vauxhall on 8th July 1950 with a Waterloo to Farnborough special, hauling air-braked Eastern Region stock.

R. C. Riley

Plate 27: A Stephenson Locomotive Society special, headed by No. 32337, with a train of crimson and cream stock, approaches Partridge Green on the Steyning line on 23rd June 1956.

R. C. Riley

Plate 28: A Brighton-bound goods train approaches Arundel Junction, after passing through Ford Station, behind No. 32343.

Author's Collection

Plate 29: A rather dirty No. 32344, still with 'British Railways' on the tender, passes through Redhill with a Brighton to Bricklayers Arms parcel train on 25th June 1951.

Brian Morrison

Plate 30: On 23rd March 1957, No. 32349, at the head of a Salisbury to Portsmouth goods train, passes Eastleigh Locomotive Works' erecting shop, where for many years this class returned for repairs.

L. Elsey

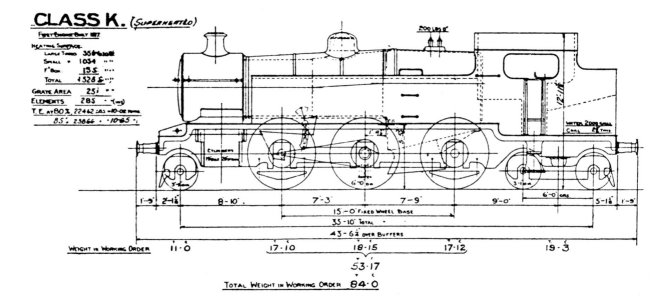

Figure 2: Maunsell, shortly after taking office in 1913 on the SECR, produced a design for a passenger 2-6-4T K class locomotive, interchangeable with his tender design. The prototype appeared in June 1917.

No. A790 was thoroughly tested and was generally successful, although water shortage was sometimes experienced on the longer runs to the Kent Coast.

No other member of the class was ordered until after the formation of the Southern Railway, when an order for twenty was placed. Nine of these, Nos. A791-9 were built by Armstrong Whitworth & Co. and ten were built at Brighton, Nos. A800-9, all parts being supplied by Ashford Works and the boilers by the North British Locomotive Co. The remaining locomotive was to become the 3-cylinder tank, No. A890 *River Frome*, to be built in 1925 (*see Figure 6*). The class were named after rivers in the south. Some modifications were made to Nos. A791-809, which differed from No. A790 in hav-

ing laminated springs to the bissel truck and bogie, increased, superheat, regulator in the dome instead of the smokebox.

Serious complaints came from engine crews, particularly on the Central Section, who did not appreciate the tendency to roll heavily and unexpectedly on indifferent track when at speed. This came to a head after several derailments when, on 24th August 1927, No. A800 *River Cray*, whilst working a Cannon Street to Deal express, became derailed near Sevenoaks, colliding with a bridge abutment. The train was completely wrecked; thirteen lives were lost and forty passengers badly injured.

Trial running was carried out on both the LNER and SR main lines, and it was decided that the complete class should be withdrawn. They were subsequently converted to 2-6-0 tender engines, thereby becoming a part of the U class, this being the reason for including these 2-6-4T locomotives in this publication.

Summary of the Maunsell 2-Cylinder K class Locomotive

Loco No.	Name	Built	Works No.	Date Built	Converted to U class	Date Withdrawn
A790	*River Avon*	Ashford	--	6/17	Eastleigh 6/28	5/65
A791	*River Adur*	A.W. & Co.	761	5/25	Eastleigh 7/28	6/66
A792	*River Arun*	A.W. & Co.	762	5/25	Eastleigh 7/28	9/64
A793	*River Ouse*	A.W. & Co.	763	5/25	Eastleigh 6/28	5/64
A794	*River Rother*	A.W. & Co.	764	5/25	Eastleigh 6/28	6/63
A795	*River Medway*	A.W. & Co.	765	6/25	Eastleigh 6/28	6/63
A796	*River Stour*	A.W. & Co.	766	6/25	Eastleigh 7/28	1/64
A797	*River Mole*	A.W. & Co.	767	6/25	Ashford 6/28	1/64
A798	*River Wey*	A.W. & Co.	768	6/25	Ashford 8/28	9/64
A799	*River Test*	A.W. & Co.	769	6/25	Ashford 7/28	2/65
A800	*River Cray*	Brighton	—	7/26	Ashford 12/28	10/65
A801	*River Darenth*	Brighton	—	7/26	Ashford 7/28	6/64
A802	*River Cuckmere*	Brighton	—	8/26	Ashford 7/28	9/64
A803	*River Itchen*	Brighton	—	8/26	Brighton 6/28	3/66
A804	*River Tamar*	Brighton	—	9/26	Brighton 6/28	6/64
A805	*River Camel*	Brighton	—	10/26	Ashford 3/28	7/63
A806	*River Torridge*	Brighton	—	10/26	Brighton 6/28	1/64
A807	*River Axe*	Brighton	—	11/26	Brighton 6/28	1/64
A808	*River Char*	Brighton	—	11/26	Brighton 7/28	1/64
A809	*River Dart*	Brighton	—	12/26	Brighton 7/28	1/66

Plate 31: K class 2-6-4T No. 790, as built, in SECR grey livery, stands outside Tonbridge Shed on 31st May 1919.
LCGB, Ken Nunn Collection

Plate 32: No. 790, pictured near Grove Park with a Cannon Street to Tonbridge train in 1919.
Author's Collection

Plate 33: No. A790 in Southern Railway passenger livery, in August 1924, with the SECR cast plate on the bunker and a larger diameter chimney.
National Railway Museum

Plate 34: No. A792 *River Arun*, fitted with dual brakes for working Central Section air-braked stock, stands outside Brighton Shed early in 1926.

Author's Collection

Plate 35: Making a fine sight heading the 'down' 'Southern Belle' all Pullman train on the Quarry line, near Merstham, in 1926, is No. A790 *River Avon*.

Lens of Sutton

Plate 36: No. A806 *River Torridge* prepares to leave the shed, early in 1927. Nos. A800-9 were only fitted with the vacuum brake, and during their short lives as tank engines were mainly allocated to Redhill, working over the Reading line. One could be seen daily hauling the heavy Birkenhead to Dover through train.

Lens of Sutton

Plate 37:   On 26th August 1925, No. A792 *River Arun* hauls a Victoria to Brighton train on the Quarry line, near Merstham.

Lens of Sutton

Plate 38:   No. A794, formerly *River Rother* but now rebuilt to a 2-6-0, heads a Victoria to Eastbourne train and passes Copyhold Junction in 1929. The double track diverging to the right joined the line now used by the Bluebell Railway at Horsted Keynes which closed to passenger traffic in 1963, and was subsequently cut back to Ardingly and made single track to serve a roadstone concentration depot with block trains from the Somerset quarries.

Author's Collection

Plate 39: No. A802 heads an 'up' train past Honor Oak Park Station in April 1931.

Photomatic

Plate 40: Running light down the Brighton main line is No. A796, photographed shortly after its rebuilding. This was one of the ten 'River' tanks (Nos. A790-9) to retain the Westinghouse brake for use on the Central Section to work Brighton and Eastbourne trains. It also clearly shows the cab, which differed from the U class in having a cutaway portion of the side sheets extended into the curvature of the roof. The 'River' names were not retained on rebuilding, due to the adverse publicity after the derailments, finally ending with the Sevenoaks disaster in 1927.

Author's Collection

Plate 41: No. 1806, now fitted with smoke deflectors, painted lined green and with front buffer beam footsteps, is seen about to leave Waterloo with a stopping train for Portsmouth in 1938.

Photomatic

Plate 42: Ex-works and in plain black with Bulleid-style numbers and lettering, No. 1795 is seen at Ashford on 6th July 1946 fitted with a U1 type chimney. It still retains the smokebox snifting valves but has the piston tail rods removed.

R. C. Riley

Plate 43: No. 31802 is pictured on Ashford Shed on 22nd June 1951. This locomotive is in plain black livery, with British Railways lettering and numerals on the cab and buffer beam in yellow-shaded green, also a smokebox numberplate. This treatment occurred quite often if the locomotive entered works for minor repairs not entailing a repaint. In early BR days the smokebox numberplate was fitted.

L. Elsey

Plate 44: Standing on the boiler wash-out road in Yeovil Shed, on 10th July 1956, is No. 31794. This class was quite popular with West Country enginemen. Nos. 1790-5 were stationed at Yeovil from 1933 to 1958.

R. C. Riley

Plate 45: No. 31790 prepares to leave Exeter (St. David's) for Exeter (Central) unaided, with a Plymouth to Exeter (Central) train on 19th July 1958. It was most unusual to see a U class working west of Exeter, via Okehampton, although they had been seen passing through Teignmouth on the regular SR/WR crew exchange trips.

R. C. Riley

CROSS-COUNTRY

Plate 46: No. 31805, with a Bristol to Portsmouth train, approaches Fareham on 2nd August 1953. This locomotive has a 4,000 gallon tender but no BR emblem; a situation which occurred quite often at that time when transfers were not available when repainted in early BR days.

Author's Collection

Plate 47: During the last few weeks of the summer service, on 5th September 1953, with a 'Saturday only' working, No. 31796 heads a mixed collection of LMS carmine and cream and GWR chocolate and cream coaches with a Portsmouth to Cardiff train, and is seen leaving Southampton Central.

L. Elsey

LIVERY VARIATIONS

Plate 48: No. 31801, pictured on 16th October 1960, on Eastleigh Shed. It is fitted with the BR a.w.s., and the vacuum reservoir and battery box are on the right-hand running plate. Note the prominent sand box filler in front of the leading splasher. The power classification, 4P/4F, is above the cab number and the yellow dot denotes the water treatment. In 1964, when lines West of Salisbury were transferred to the Western Region, the yellow dot was altered to a triangle to avoid confusion with the route classification on Westen Region locomotives.

L. Elsey

Plate 49: No. 31803 is pictured with a 4,000 gallon tender. Note the difference in the lining around cab and tender, and also the size of the numerals (possibly hand-painted) compared with those of No. 31801 (*Plate 48*) which has the standard BR 8in numerals.

L. Elsey

Plate 50: Another cab lining variation, and the latest BR crest on the tender, seen on No. 31791 at Eastleigh on 7th September 1960. Latest modifications include new cylinders and front end frames. The small box on the footplate above the cylinders houses the anti-vacuum valve. A BR Class 4 chimney and modified blast pipe has been fitted but no 25kV electrification signs are visible.

L. Elsey

Plate 51: The RCTS Longmoor railtour is pictured, on 30th April 1966, about to leave Windsor & Eton (Riverside) Station for Waterloo, headed by the last two U class locomotives in revenue-earning service, Nos. 31791 and 31639.

C. Elsey

Plate 52: On the closing day of passenger services on the Didcot, Newbury & Southampton line, 5th March 1960, the fireman of No. 31794 takes the single line token before Worthy Down. This locomotive returned later in the day from Didcot with a train of empty oil tank wagons for Fawley Refinery.

L. Elsey

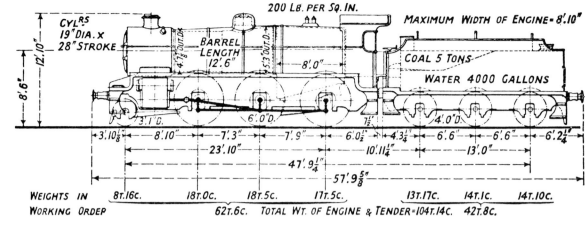

200 LB. PER SQ. IN.

MAXIMUM WIDTH OF ENGINE = 8'. 10"

CYL^RS 19" DIA. X 28" STROKE

BARREL LENGTH 12'. 6"

COAL 5 TONS

WATER 4000 GALLONS

WEIGHTS IN WORKING ORDER

8T.16C. 18T.0C. 18T.5C. 17T.5C. 13T.17C. 14T.1C. 14T.10C.

62T.6C. TOTAL WT. OF ENGINE & TENDER = 104T.14C. 42T.8C.

HEATING SURFACE, TUBES—	SUPERHEATER ELEMENTS ... ... 21-1¼ IN. DIA. OUTS.
LARGE AND SMALL ... ... 1,390·6 SQ. FT.	LARGE TUBES ... ... 21-5⅛ IN. DIA. OUTS. ⎫ 12 FT. 10 ¹³⁄₁₆ IN.
FIREBOX ... ... 135·0 ,,	SMALL TUBES ... ... 173-1¾ IN. DIA. OUTS. ⎬ BET. TUBEPLATES
TOTAL (EVAPORATIVE) ... ... 1,525·6 ,,	GRATE AREA ... ... 25·0 SQ. FT.
SUPERHEATER ... ... 285·0 ,,	TRACTIVE EFFORT (AT 85 PER CENT. B.P.) ... 23,866 LB.
COMBINED HEATING SURFACES ... ... 1,810·6 ,,	

Figure 3: The drawing depicts the later 4,000 gallon tender with turned-in top, built with Nos. A630-9 in 1931.

The U class engines were designed with 6ft. driving wheels, otherwise interchangeable with N class parts. Initially, twenty engines, Nos. A610-29 were built with 3,500 gallon tenders in 1928/9. Ten more, Nos. A630-9, were built with 4,000 gallon tenders in 1931. During their life, various modifications were carried out to the class including tender changes, for various reasons, and this included the 'River' class rebuilds, Nos. A790-809, making the class up to fifty in total. The rebuilds could be distinguished by a lower running plate with splashers over the driving wheels, and cab side sheets cut away extending into the cab roof, and retaining the double spectacle in the cab front.

The entire class were painted in the Southern Railway passenger livery when built, retaining this until during World War II when it was painted plain black. On nationalisation, before any decisions had been made with regard to livery style, two members of the class carried the 'S' prefix (Nos. 1620 from March to September 1948 and No. 1631 from February 1948 to November 1949).

From 1955, a number of the class had new cylinders with outside steam pipes, similar to the work done on the N class, and also leading frame replacements. In some cases where the main frames were in a poor condition, new frames were fitted.

Commencing with No. 31806 in November 1957, BR Standard Class 4 chimneys and modified blast pipes were applied to some members of the class.

Four of the class have been preserved; Nos. 1618 and 1638 on the Bluebell Railway and Nos. 31625 and 31806 on the Mid-Hants Railway, although restoration has not yet been completed on all of them.

Summary of the Maunsell 2-Cylinder U class Locomotives

Loco. No.	Built	Date Built	Date Withdrawn	Loco. No.	Built	built	Date Withdrawn
A610	Brighton	8/28	12/62	A625	Ashford	3/29	1/64
A611	Brighton	8/28	10/63	A626	Ashford	3/29	1/64
A612	Brighton	7/28	5/63	A627	Ashford	4/29	10/65
A613	Brighton	6/28	1/64	A628	Ashford	4/29	6/64
A614	Brighton	7/28	11/63	A629	Ashford	12/29	1/64
A615	Brighton	8/28	10/63	A630	Ashford	2/31	11/62
A616	Brighton	9/28	6/64	A631	Ashford	3/31	9/63
A617	Brighton	10/28	1/64	A632	Ashford	3/31	9/64
A618	Brighton	10/28	1/64	A633	Ashford	3/31	12/63
A619	Brighton	12/28	12/65	A634	Ashford	4/31	12/63
A620	Ashford	11/28	4/65	A635	Ashford	4/31	12/63
A621	Ashford	12/28	6/64	A636	Ashford	4/31	6/63
A622	Ashford	1/29	1/64	A637	Ashford	5/31	8/63
A623	Ashford	1/29	12/63	A638	Ashford	5/31	1/64
A624	Ashford	2/29	6/64	A639	Ashford	5/31	6/66

Plate 53: No. A611 as built in 1928, about to leave Clapham Yard with empty coaching stock for Waterloo in August 1931. When new, Nos. A610-24 were shedded at Guildford.
Photomatic

Plate 54: A fine side view action shot of No. A635 heading for the Kent Coast, shortly after being built.
Author's Collection

Plate 55: A July 1939 view at Southampton Central showing No. 1624 in Southern Railway livery about to leave with a Portsmouth Harbour to Cardiff train. The locomotive still has piston tail rods and a U1 chimney.

L. Elsey

Plate 56: No. 1635 heads a Bricklayers Arms to Guildford goods train west of Sutton in the early 1930s. Although the locomotive has had 1,000 added to its number under the 1931 renumbering scheme, it has not received smoke deflectors, a modification which commenced during the same year.

Lens of Sutton

Plate 57: In full cry with a loaded train for Tongham gasworks, No. 1622 passes Ash Junction in the early 1950s. This line from Ash Junction to Farnham Junction was signalled as a main line, although the latter junction had been disused for many years. In the mid-1950s, the line as far as Tongham was reduced to siding status.

Author's Collection

Plate 58: No. 31629 undergoes a periodical examination of coupling rods and pistons at Bricklayers Arms repair shops on 11th September 1954.

Brian Morrison

Plate 59: On 11th April 1954, a stopping train from Salisbury to Portsmouth, having just left Bursledon and crossed the River Hamble behind No. 31638, makes a run at the bank up to Swanwick, which has a ruling gradient of 1 in 81 for most of the way.

L. Elsey

PULVERISED FUEL

Plate 60: No. A629, pictured on Eastbourne Shed, fitted for pulverised fuel burning on 20th February 1932. This was a German design, fitted at Ashford Works in December 1929. The 3,500 gallon tender was modified to carry a large covered hopper, so reducing the water capacity to 3,300 gallons. The hopper fed fuel first via screws driven by steam and then forced by air through piping to the firebox. The blast of air was created by a steam turbine fan which was mounted at the rear of the covered hopper on top of the tender. A secondary feed was provided by a belt, driven by a steam engine for lighting-up purposes. This entered at the rear of the firebox, whereas the main feeds were at the side. The lower firebox was fire brick-lined, with no fire bars where most of the combustion took place. The tender had a small cab fitted to keep the cab dust free when bunkering.

H. C. Casserley/S. C. Nash Collection

Plate 61: A rear view of the tender of No. A629, pictured on 20th February 1932, showing the covered fuel hopper with the steam turbine fan casing mounted on the top of the tender.

H. C. Casserley

Plate 62: No. A629 working a test train whilst stationed at Eastbourne. Apparently, when running, large quantities of partly-consumed fuel were violently ejected from the chimney, and in an endeavour to clear these fiery missiles from the leading coaches, smoke deflectors were fitted in October 1931 at Brighton.

A. L. P. Reavil Collection/NRM

Plate 63: No. A629 on Eastbourne Shed, on 5th August 1932, together with SECR No.751 which, although an ex-LBSC 'Terrier' tank which was bought by the SECR in 1904 for the Isle of Sheppey Light Railway, was eventually sent to Eastbourne to provide steam for the hoist to the pulverised fuel hopper, seen in the background. No. A629 ran trials for two years with no notable success, or with any fuel savings over conventional coal burning. The locomotive returned to Ashford Works in October 1932, where the covered hopper apparatus was removed and it returned to traffic as No. 1629 in December 1932 as a standard U class engine.

H. F. Wheeller

OIL BURNING

Plate 64: No. 1797, fitted for oil burning, on Fratton Shed and photographed on 11th September 1948. As part of the abortive post-war Government oil-burning conversion scheme, caused by a post-war coal shortage, two U class locomotives, Nos. 1797 and 1625, were converted at Ashford Works, entering service in this form in October and December 1947 respectively. Further engines of the class were earmarked for conversion and work was in hand on No. 1629 when the scheme was abandoned. Electric lighting was fitted to both engines, the turbo generator being fitted behind the left-hand smoke deflector on the running plate. No. 1625 lost the 4,000 gallon tender, which was replaced by one of normal 3,500 capacity to ensure the fuel tanks were within the loading gauge. Both engines worked from Fratton and Exmouth Junction sheds with some success, and fuelling points were installed at Eastleigh and Exmouth Junction. Both locomotives were reconverted to coal burning in December 1948.

H. C. Casserley

Plate 65: Also on Fratton Shed on the same day, 11th September 1948, was No. 1625, showing a rear view the oil fuel tank and electric lighting for the headcodes. The livery was all black with Bulleid-style lettering. O the next road in front of No. 1625 is an oil-burning Class T9 4-4-0, which lasted in this condition for as long as tl Moguls.

H. C. Casserle

Plate 66: The 4.50p.m. Southampton Terminus to Andover Junction train leaves Millbrook, on 1st May 1962, headed by No. 31639.

L. Elsey

Plate 67: No. 31634 is pictured on a Southampton Terminus van train on the 'down' slow line south of Shawford Station on 12th August 1962.

L. Elsey

Plate 68: Evening time at Salisbury, and No. 31620 shunts wagons prior to leaving with a freight for the West Country on 12th May 1958.

Brian Morrison

Plate 69: On 10th February 1963, two unidentified U class locomotives double-head a troop train, formed of LMS stock, to Bulford Camp, near Newton Tony. Double-heading was necessary on the branch due to gradients of 1 in 60 out of Amesbury. Passenger traffic to Bulford ceased in June 1952, but the line remained open for freight and military specials to Bulford Camp, with the branch finally closing in March 1963.

L. Elsey

Plate 70: No. 31638 in its final form, at Eastleigh Shed on 10th June 1963, with only seven months service to go before withdrawal from BR service.

L. Elsey

Plate 71: On 12th August 1951, No. 31636, is seen in early British Railways livery of plain black with Bulleid style shaded lettering.

L. Elsey

Plate 72: No. 31635, at Eastleigh, on 10th June 1963, showing a U class locomotive with all the modifications fitted — new cylinders, anti-vacuum valve above the cylinders, new front end framing, BR Standard Class 4 chimney and blast pipe, 25kV electrification warning flashes on the smoke deflectors, and firebox, water treatment indicated by the yellow dot on the cab and BR a.w.s.

L. Elsey

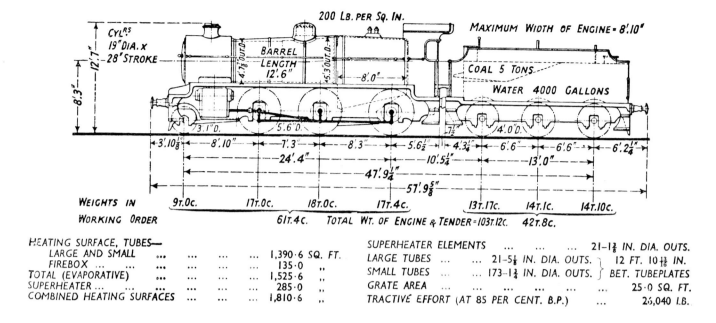

Figure 4: This drawing depicts the last batch of N class locomotives, Nos. 1400-14 with 4,000 gallon turned-in top tenders, and U1-style chimneys.

The N class was one of Maunsell's new locomotive designs for the SECR, which was delayed by the advent of World War I, the prototype, No. 810, appearing from Ashford Works in July 1917.

No. 810 was finished in the usual SECR grey livery, running trials between Ashford and Tonbridge after which it was allocated to Bricklayers Arms for the heavy Richborough goods traffic which, up until then, had to be double-headed with C class 0-6-0s. A more powerful locomotive was also required for mixed traffic purposes.

Because of a heavy backlog of repair work, No. 811 did not appear until June 1920, and was the first of a batch of fifteen, the last, No. A825, being completed in December 1923. To give employment after the Armistice, Woolwich Arsenal produced complete parts for N class locomotives, except boilers which were supplied by the North British Locomotive Co. and assembled at Ashford as Nos. A826-75 in 1924 and 1925. A further batch was built, Nos. 1400-14, at Ashford from 1932 to 1934. From No. 1407 onwards, they had left-hand drive and smoke deflectors. The rest of the class were fitted with smoke deflectors as they passed through works from 1933 onwards. Smokebox snifting valves were removed by 1948, this fitting being removed from all Southern Railway locomotives at the same time. The last member of the class to be withdrawn was No. 31408, in June 1966, although No. 31874 is preserved on the Mid-Hants Railway (*see Plate 157*).

Summary of the Maunsell 2-cylinder N class Locomotives

Loco. No.	Built	Date Built	Date Withdrawn	Loco. No.	Built	Date Built	Date Withdrawn
810	Ashford	8/17	3/64	822 was fitted with three cylinders, see the later N1 class			
811	Ashford	6/20	7/65	823	Ashford	5/23	9/63
812	Ashford	8/20	7/64	824	Ashford	8/23	10/63
813	Ashford	9/20	10/63	A825	Ashford	12/23	8/63
814	Ashford	11/20	7/64	A826	Woolwich Arsenal/ Ashford	6/24	8/63
815	Ashford	12/20	5/63	A827	Woolwich Arsenal/ Ashford	5/24	6/64
816	Ashford	1/22	1/66	A828	Woolwich Arsenal/ Ashford	6/24	9/64
817	Ashford	1/22	1/64	A829	Woolwich Arsenal/ Ashford	7/24	1/64
818	Ashford	3/22	9/63	A830	Woolwich Arsenal/ Ashford	6/24	1/64
819	Ashford	5/22	1/64	A831	Woolwich Arsenal/ Ashford	6/24	4/65
820	Ashford	8/22	8/63	A832	Woolwich Arsenal/ Ashford	7/24	1/64
821	Ashford	10/22	5/64	A833	Woolwich Arsenal/ Ashford	7/24	2/64

Loco. No.	Built	Date Built	Date Withdrawn	Loco. No.	Built	Date Built	Date Withdrawn
A834	Woolwich Arsenal/ Ashford	7/24	9/64	A863	Woolwich Arsenal/ Ashford	5/25	7/63
A835	Woolwich Arsenal/ Ashford	7/24	9/64	A864	Woolwich Arsenal/ Ashford	6/25	1/64
A836	Woolwich Arsenal/ Ashford	7/24	12/63	A865	Woolwich Arsenal/ Ashford	6/25	8/63
A837	Woolwich Arsenal/ Ashford	7/24	9/64	A866	Woolwich Arsenal/ Ashford	5/25	1/66*
A838	Woolwich Arsenal/ Ashford	7/24	2/64	A867	Woolwich Arsenal/ Ashford	7/25	7/63
A839	Woolwich Arsenal/ Ashford	7/24	12/63	A868	Woolwich Arsenal/ Ashford	7/25	1/64
A840	Woolwich Arsenal/ Ashford	8/24	9/64	A869	Woolwich Arsenal/ Ashford	7/25	8/64
A841	Woolwich Arsenal/ Ashford	8/24	3/64	A870	Woolwich Arsenal/ Ashford	7/25	4/64
A842	Woolwich Arsenal/ Ashford	8/24	9/65	A871	Woolwich Arsenal/ Ashford	7/25	12/63
A843	Woolwich Arsenal/ Ashford	8/24	9/64	A872	Woolwich Arsenal/ Ashford	8/25	5/63
A844	Woolwich Arsenal/ Ashford	9/24	12/63	A873	Woolwich Arsenal/ Ashford	9/25	1/66
A845	Woolwich Arsenal/ Ashford	9/24	9/64	A874	Woolwich Arsenal/ Ashford	9/25	3/64
A846	Woolwich Arsenal/ Ashford	1/25	9/64	A875	Woolwich Arsenal/ Ashford	8/25	8/64
A847	Woolwich Arsenal/ Ashford	2/25	9/63	1400	Ashford	7/32	6/64
A848	Woolwich Arsenal/ Ashford	2/25	2/64	1401	Ashford	8/32	7/65
A849	Woolwich Arsenal/ Ashford	2/25	7/64	1402	Ashford	8/32	8/63
A850	Woolwich Arsenal/ Ashford	2/25	1/64	1403	Ashford	8/32	6/63
A851	Woolwich Arsenal/ Ashford	2/25	8/63	1404	Ashford	10/32	12/63
A852	Woolwich Arsenal/ Ashford	3/25	9/63	1405	Ashford	11/32	6/66
A853	Woolwich Arsenal/ Ashford	4/25	9/64	1406	Ashford	1/33	9/64
A854	Woolwich Arsenal/ Ashford	3/25	6/64	1407	Ashford	8/33	7/63
A855	Woolwich Arsenal/ Ashford	3/25	9/64	1408	Ashford	9/33	6/66
A856	Woolwich Arsenal/ Ashford	3/25	7/64	1409	Ashford	10/33	11/62
A857	Woolwich Arsenal/ Ashford	4/25	1/64	1410	Ashford	11/33	11/64
A858	Woolwich Arsenal/ Ashford	5/25	12/65	1411	Ashford	11/33	4/66
A859	Woolwich Arsenal/ Ashford	4/25	9/64	1412	Ashford	12/33	8/64
A860	Woolwich Arsenal/ Ashford	4/25	10/63	1413	Ashford	1/34	6/64
A861	Woolwich Arsenal/ Ashford	6/25	5/63	1414	Ashford	1/34	11/62
A862	Woolwich Arsenal/ Ashford	5/25	4/65				

This engine, as Southern No. 866, was exhibited at the British Empire Exhibition at Wembley from May to November 1925.

Plate 73: Prototype N class, No. 810, in SECR grey livery, with large white numerals on the tender, buffer beam, cast cab plate, and piston tail rods, as built in 1917.

Author's Collection

Plate 74: No. 818, running in 1924, and fitted with a stovepipe chimney which was previously carried by No. 819. Nos. 812/817 were also fitted with the same type of chimney. By April 1927, standard N class chimneys were provided in all cases. Apparently, there was no reason for the fitting of these stovepipe chimneys, although in the first half of 1922, the erecting shop at Ashford had a shortage of chimneys.

Tony Sedgewick Collection

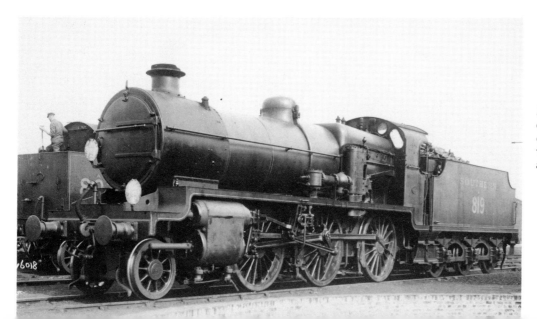

Plate 75: During the period December 1924 to April 1927, No. A819 carried a Worthington feed pump fitted on the left-hand footplate, and also a U1-type chimney.

E. W. Fry Collection

EPSOM RACES

Plate 76: No. 820 in 1920 with a race special, near Kingswood, on the Tattenham Corner branch, formed of Pullman cars in the SECR lake livery.
Lens of Sutton

Plate 77: A race special formed of an assortment of rolling stock, is headed by No. 819, with a stovepipe chimney, near Kingswood in May 1923.

Lens of Sutton

Plate 78: No. 1863 climbs towards Kingswood with an all Pullman race special shortly after being renumbered under the 1931 scheme, in which all ex-SECR locomotives had a 1,000 added to their numbers in place of the prefix 'A' for Ashford.
Lens of Sutton

Plate 79: Exmouth Junction Shed, and No. 1406 a few months after being built at Ashford in May 1933. Smoke deflectors had not been fitted at the time of building although some Moguls were so fitted in 1933.

Author's Collection

Plate 80: Nos. A857 and A849 leave Exeter (St. David's) in preparation to tackle the 1 in 37 incline to Exeter (Central) in the late 1920s.

Author's Collection

Plate 81: No. 1823 is seen shortly after receiving smoke deflectors in 1933. Some locomotives had round hand-holds high up, whereas some had rectangular hand-holds lower down. No. 1823 still retains the original chimney and piston tail rods.

Author's Collection

Plate 82: On 21st May 1939 at Ashford Works, No. 1844 is being overhauled and is resplendent in the Southern Railway passenger livery with the oval cast cab plate. This was rather unusual as the Bulleid-style livery cab numerals and 'Southern' on the tender were applied from late 1938.

Tony Sedgewick Collection

Plate 83: No. 1412 poses with a breakdown train in 1937. Of the final series of N class locomotives, Nos. 1400-14, those from No. 1407 upwards were built with smoke deflectors and left-hand drive. During 1937/8, these locomotives received new 4,000 gallon tenders with fireman's fittings correctly sited to suit the left-hand drive, and the original tenders built for right-hand drive were transferred to U class locomotives Nos. 1610-7.

Author's Collection

EARLY BRITISH RAILWAYS LIVERIES

Plate 84 (above): No. s1825 in plain black, with the cab numerals and tender lettering in Bulleid-style, and no smokebox numberplate. It is pictured at Brighton in April 1948 and the locomotive was renumbered to 31825 in March 1951.

R. C. Riley

Plate 85 (right): Standing in the yard at Ashford Works, in September 1946, is No. 1854, painted in lined malachite green livery with '31854' on the tender. It was repainted in the lined black livery in July 1950. There were only two N class locomotives painted in malachite green, the other being No. 1817, which was repainted in May 1949.

Tony Sedgewick Collection

Plate 86: No. 31821, awaiting to enter Ashford Works for repairs on 3rd June 1951. The locomotive is painted in the lined black livery, with yellow Gill Sans style numbers and lettering, which was rather unusual in the early years of nationalisation.

L. Elsey

EXPERIMENTAL WORK

Plate 87: Fitted with Marshall valve gear, No. 1850 is pictured at Eastleigh Works in February 1934. It ran trials on the Western Section main line, and at slow speeds the Marshall valve gear behaved very well and showed marked improvement economically over the Walschaerts valve gear, but at 50-55m.p.h. it developed an unpleasant knock, which suggested it was unsuitable for passenger train work. However, No. 1850 was rostered for a Basingstoke to Waterloo semi-fast working on 22nd March 1934 with the result that the right-hand valve gear disintegrated at speed near Woking. Two days later, the engine arrived at Brighton Works for reconversion to a standard N class, and returned to traffic on 11th April 1934.

Tony Sedgewick Collection

Plate 88: No. 1850, seen in Eastleigh paint shop, in February 1934, with Marshall valve gear and indicator shelters for trials on the Western Section.

Author's Collection

Plate 89: No. A816 in Eastleigh paint shop in m[...] 1930, fitted with a steam conservation system, [...] vented by a Glasgow marine draughtsman, whi[...] consisted principally of a condenser on marine ty[...] principles with circulating pumps. It involved exte[...] sive alterations and a year's work before the engi[...] was ready for trials, and this picture shows the loc[...] motive fitted with a square chimney during t[...] experiments which lasted several years.

Author's Collect[...]

Plate 90 (below): In the erecting shop at Eastleigh is No. A816, with a normal chimney and a fan fitted on the smokebox door which provided the firebox draught. This view shows the right-hand side with the condenser tank and circulating pumps.

Lens of Sutton

Plate 91 (below): This view of No. A816 shows the left-hand side and some of the pumps; the locomotive having been repainted before going to trials.

Lens of Sutton

Plate 92 (below): A side view of No. A816 in its final form, the cab and tender having been touched up, presumably for publicity purposes. The main exhaust from the cylinders was led through the side of the smokebox into the condenser tank, with a non-return valve to prevent the water entering the cylinders. It was suggested that the experiment failed owing to poor draughting arrangements and back pressure set up by the condensing system, which made it impossible to give a standard N class performance. The locomotive reverted to normal as No. 1816 in August 1935.

Author's Collection

Plate 93: No. 1831, fitted for oil burning, awaiting the road at Eastleigh in February 1948. This locomotive was converted to oil firing in June 1947 at Ashford Works, and after trials was put into service at Exmouth Junction in September of that year. Nos. 1830 and 1859 were earmarked for similar modifications but work never commenced. Electric lighting was fitted at Eastleigh Works in January 1948. Reconversion to coal burning was carried out at Ashford in December 1948.

L. Elsey

Plate 94: Passing Cosham with an Eastleigh to Fratton freight train, on 13th March 1948, is No. 1831, fitted for oil burning.

P. C. Short

Plate 95: Putting on steam to climb the 1 in 103 bank to Sway, No. 31818 passes Lymington Junction, on 14th October 1961, with a freight mainly composed of empty tank wagons returning to Furzebrook Sidings on the Swanage branch.

L. Elsey

Plate 96: No. 31825 passes Eastleigh South Junction with a Salisbury to Fratton freight on 16th January 1954.

L. Elsey

Plate 97: Having been released from the buffer stops by the departure of the 17.40 London Bridge to Newhaven train, on 25th June 1952, No. 31853 awaits to return for empty stock to work to the carriage sidings.

Brian Morrison

Plate 98: On a bright September morning in 1957, No. 31820 makes a rousing attack on the 1 in 64 bank to Grosvenor Bridge, over the River Thames, with a Victoria to Ramsgate train.

R. C. Riley

Plate 99: Pullman cars make a prestige load as No. 31824, heading the 'down' 'Kentish Belle', passes Factory Junction, Stewarts Lane, on 23rd August 1958. Battersea Power-Station can be seen in the background, and the line to Stewarts Lane motive power depot is on the left. On summer Saturdays, the 'Kentish Belle' was an Ashford working, and presumably a Mogul was the best available power the shed could supply on this occasion.

R. C. Riley

Plate 100: A Victoria to Margate summer relief train, headed by No. 31813, passes Bickley Junction on 14th July 1951.

Brian Morrison

Plate 101: The 14.02 (SO) Portsmouth Harbour to Sheffield (Midland) through train, headed by No. 31873, passes through Otter-bourne Cutting, near Shawford, in September 1963. The train is composed of a mixture of Gresley and BR Mk. I stock, all in ma-roon livery.

L. Elsey

Plate 102: No. 31872 leaves Southampton Central on a rather dull Saturday, 7th July 1951, with a Portsmouth Harbour to Ilfra-combe through train composed of Bulleid stock.

L. Elsey

Plate 103: The 12.01 Eastbourne to Manchester through train passes Kensington Olympia, on 18th August 1956, with No. 31817 in charge. The engine change will be carried out at Willesden. In the background there is an ex-LSWR Class M7, No. 30249, and two ex-LNER B1 class locomotives, showing the variety of motive power that could be seen on the West London line, especially on summer Saturdays.

R. C. Riley

Plate 104: A budding young railway enthusiast watches the trains go and enjoys the last days of steam before complete electrification, as No. 31405 passes Bickley with a 'down' Ramsgate train on 5th August 1957.

R. C. Riley

Plate 105: A pleasant view, in wintry sunshine, of No. 31404 traversing the Chiselhurst loop line with an 'up' coal train on 20th February 1953.

Brian Morrison

Plate 106: On 19th July 1959, No. 31813 heads an Engineer's train which is returning to Eastleigh permanent way depot after weekend work between Chandler's Ford and Eastleigh. This line, between Eastleigh and Romsey, is now singled, and is mainly a freight only line, although two regular summer (SO) trains work over it and it is also used whenever there are any main line diversions.

Tony Molyneaux

Plate 107: No. 31831 finds the going hard when tackling the 1 in 100 climb out of Blackboy Tunnel, near Exmouth Junction, with a Sunday permanent way Engineer's train on 11th May 1958.

Brian Morrison

Plate 108: On 5th May 1964, in the West Country, No. 31849 climbs from Boscarne Junction to Bodmin (General), assisted by another member of the class, No. 31840 at the rear as it heads a Wenford to Lostwithiel china clay train.

S. C. Nash

Plate 109: Commencing in October 1955, new cylinders with outside steam pipes, and new front frames, were being fitted to all Mogul classes if required at Ashford Works. No. 31848, the first Mogul so converted, ran minus smoke deflectors for fourteen months, eventually receiving them in December 1956.

Author's Collection

Plate 110: Two N class locomotives at Exmouth Junction Shed, on 17th July 1960, await their next turn of duty. The locomotives differ as No. 31835 has been fitted with new cylinders, a cover above, housing the anti-vacuum valve and the new curved top front framing. No. 31841 is in the original condition and both locomotives are fitted with BR a.w.s. The receiver magnet protection plate below the buffer beam shows this and both engines also carry BR Class 4 chimneys.

Tony Molyneaux

Plate 111: On 20th September 1964, ex-works Mogul No. 31816 is pictured at Eastleigh. It is in its final condition but still retains the original cylinders and frames, U1 chimney, BR a.w.s., battery box and reservoir on the right-hand footplate in front of the cab, and water treatment.

L. Elsey

CENTRAL SECTION SPECIAL WORKINGS

Plate 112 (above): A special train, seen east of Rowfant on the Three Bridges to East Grinstead line in the mid-1950s. It is double-headed by N class No. 31829 and U1 class No. 31894.

Author's Collection

Plate 113 (right): On 27th February 1960, a train of empty ballast hopper wagons from Tonbridge approaches Redhill behind No. 31865. The locomotive has a repainted smokebox and red-backed numberplate.

R. C. Riley

Plate 114 (left): On 6th December 1965, No. 31866 accelerates through Shoreham-by-Sea with an LCGB enthusiasts' special working bound for Brighton, having just traversed the Steyning line which, at that time, was under threat of closure.

L. Elsey

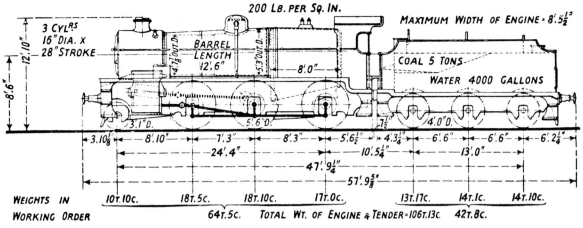

200 LB. PER SQ. IN.

3 CYL^RS
16" DIA. X
28" STROKE

12'.10"

8'.6"

BARREL LENGTH 12'.6"

4'.7⅞"OUT.D.

5'.3"OUT.D.

8'.0"

MAXIMUM WIDTH OF ENGINE = 8'.5¹⁷₃₂"

COAL 5 TONS

WATER 4000 GALLONS

3'.1"D. 5'.6"D. 7½ 4'.0"D.

3.10¹⁄₈ 8'.10" 7'.3" 8'.3" 5'.6½" 4'.3¼" 6'.6" 6'.6" 6'.2¼"
24'.4" 10'.5¼" 13'.0"
47'.9¼"
57'.9⅝"

WEIGHTS IN WORKING ORDER

10T.10C. 18T.5C. 18T.10C. 17T.0C. 13T.17C. 14T.1C. 14T.10C.
64T.5C. TOTAL WT. OF ENGINE & TENDER=106T.13C. 42T.8C.

HEATING SURFACE, TUBES—		
LARGE AND SMALL	1,390·6	SQ. FT.
FIREBOX	135·0	,,
TOTAL (EVAPORATIVE)	1,525·6	,,
SUPERHEATER	285·0	,,
COMBINED HEATING SURFACES	1,810·6	,,

SUPERHEATER ELEMENTS	21–1¾ IN. DIA. OUTS.	
LARGE TUBES ... ... 21–5⅛ IN. DIA. OUTS.	12 FT. 10¹³⁄₁₆ IN.	
SMALL TUBES ... ... 173–1¾ IN. DIA. OUTS.	BET. TUBEPLATES	
GRATE AREA	25·0 SQ. FT.	
TRACTIVE EFFORT (AT 85 PER CENT. B.P.) ...	27,700 LB.	

Figure 5: The drawing is of the later N1 class, Nos. A876-80, with three sets of Walschaerts valve gear.

N1 Class

Summary of the Maunsell 3-cylinder 'N1' Locomotives

Loco. No.	Built	Date Built	Date Withdrawn
A822	Ashford	3/23	11/62
A876	Ashford	3/30	11/62
A877	Ashford	4/30	11/62
A878	Ashford	4/30	11/62
A879	Ashford	4/30	11/62
A880	Ashford	11/30	11/62

Only twelve N class locomotives were completed by the Grouping and the thirteenth, No. 822, was fitted with three cylinders, the inside cylinder with Holcroft valve gear and the two outside with Walschaerts valve gear. It was also fitted with a larger chimney than that usually fitted to the later members of the class which were built in 1930. Leaving Ashford, on 19th March 1923, after running in, it was shedded at Bricklayers Arms for trials against N class No. 817 on goods and passenger trains.

The trials showed there was very little gained by having the extra cylinder performance-wise, although it did permit using smaller outside cylinders and therefore could work trains over the Hastings line, between Tonbridge and Hastings, with the restricted loading gauge through Mountifeld and Bo-Peep Tunnels. This proved to be an asset for working the heavy traffic in World War II.

Experience with the Holcroft valve gear led Maunsell to the decision to use three sets of Walschaerts valve gear on five locomotives, Nos. A876-80, built in 1930. In view of this, No. A822 was brought into line with the rest of the class, retaining the 3,500 gallon tender. The 3-cylinder engines rode more smoothly than the N class and, in fact, until the Kent Coast electrification was completed, they made use of the class on numerous summer Saturday extras to Margate and Ramsgate, their small coupled wheels making very little difference. After 1959, when the Kent Coast electrification was completed, they were transferred to Tonbridge where they carried out passenger and goods duties on the Redhill, Brighton, and other Central Section lines.

As with other superheated locomotives, the snifting valves were removed by Bulleid, while the 1930 series received U1 chimneys when the originals required replacement. Apart from this, there were very few changes to the class. They all entered BR stock in 1948 and the class was withdrawn in November 1962 under the Southern Region steam withdrawal policy.

None of the class were preserved.

Plate 115: No. 822, the prototype 3-cylinder N1 class locomotive in SECR grey livery, photographed in May 1923, with two sets of Walschaerts valve gear and Holcrofts conjugated valve gear for the inside cylinder, and a 3,500 gallon tender. The engine weighed 62 tons 15cwt. in working order, and the tender weighed 39 tons 5cwt. The total weight was 103 tons and the boiler pressure was 180p.s.i. which was later raised to 200p.s.i. in comparison to the drawing in *Figure 5.*

Author's Collection

Plate 116: No. 1822, in Southern Railway passenger livery, photographed in August 1931 after a major overhaul at Ashford Works when the Holcroft valve gear was replaced by three sets of Walschaerts valve gear. Front footsteps were provided immediately behind the buffer beam, similar to the rest of the class.

Author's Collection

Plate 117: Seventeen years later, No. 1822, now in plain black livery, has just arrived on Ashford Shed on 6th July 1948.

L. Elsey

Plate 118: No. A878 is being prepared for duty on Battersea Shed in July 1930. This locomotive entered service two months earlier, the class working mainly passenger and freight trains on the Hastings line. In this view, No. A878 still has an original SECR chimney.

Lens of Sutton

Plate 119: Posing for the camera is No. 1877 and, although now re-numbered under the 1931 scheme and fitted with a U1 chimney, at this time had no smoke deflectors.

Author's Collection

Plate 120: No. 31879, in BR lined black livery, at Hither Green on 14th April 1951. It is in rather a dirty state and has smokebox snifting valves.

L. Elsey

Plate 121: On 24th September 1955, No. 31822 awaits departure from Ashford Station with a stopping train for Hastings.
Brian Morrison

Plate 122: A 'down' Folkestone express, with No. 31877 in charge, near Shortlands Junction on a hot 27th July 1957.
R. C. Riley

Plate 123: On 30th May 1951, a much cleaner No. 31879 heads a Derby Day Pullman special from Cannon Street to Tattenham Corner, and is seen approaching London Bridge.

R. C. Riley

Plate 124: The 9.26a.m. Victoria to Ramsgate train, headed by No. 31876, passes through a typical LBSC suburban station, Denmark Hill, on 14th May 1956. The station building on the skyline was severely damaged by fire in March 1980, but was reopened in the spring of 1984. Part of the building is a public house furnished in a Railway theme.

R. C. Riley

Plate 125: On 24th June 1956, No. 31880 hauls an 'up' freight from Ashford to Bricklayers Arms, and passes Sidcup on the Dartford Loop line.

Brian Morrison

Plate 126: After mass withdrawal of the class in November 1962, under the Southern Region steam withdrawal policy, the locomotives were placed in store pending scrapping. On 15th August 1963, No. 31877 awaits entry to Eastleigh Works for cutting up; this took place a few weeks later.

L. Elsey

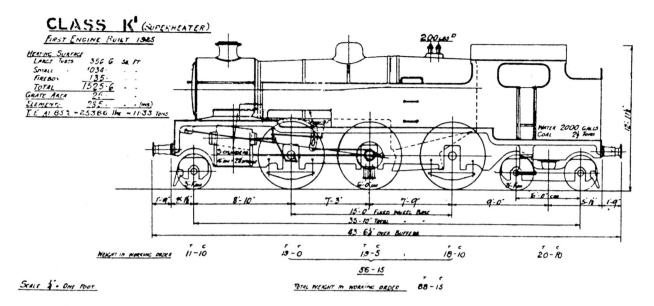

CLASS K¹ (SUPERHEATER)
FIRST ENGINE BUILT 1925

HEATING SURFACE
LARGE TUBES   356·6 SQ FT
SMALL   1034·
FIREBOX   135·
TOTAL   1525·6
GRATE AREA   25·
ELEMENTS   285·   (in³)
T.E. AT 85% = 25366 lbs = 11·33 TONS

Scale ¼" = One Foot

Total Weight in Working Order   88 - 15

Figure 6: A drawing of a K1 2-6-2T with conjugated valve gear.

K1 Class 2-6-4T

In 1925, Maunsell decided to build a 3-cylinder passenger tank identical to the K class 2-cylinder design built in 1917, the 'River' class. This engine was fitted with conjugated valve gear, similar to the N1 class, which consisted of two Walschaerts gears operating the valves on the outside cylinders, and necessary leverage to operate the middle cylinder. The wheelbase was the same as the K class. Although numbered separately, the locomotive was named *River Frome*.

The riding of the 3-cylinder tank was a source of complaint from the enginemen, and for some reason it seemed less stable than the 2-cylinder version, and was twice derailed. The second occasion was on 20th August 1927 at Bearsted, on the Maidstone East line, when seven coaches and the engine of the eleven coach train travelling at 35m.p.h. were derailed, luckily with no serious injuries to passengers or crew. Four days later, No. A800 *River Cray* was involved in a more serious accident at Sevenoaks (*see Figure 2*).

No. A890 was withdrawn together with the other 2-cylinder tanks after the Sevenoaks disaster, and was rebuilt as a 2-6-0 tender engine, and formed the prototype of the U1 class as described in *Figure 7*, the reason for including this locomotive in this publication.

Summary of the Maunsell 3-Cylinder K1 class Locomotive

Loco. No.	Name	Built	Date Built	Date converted to U1 class and works
A890	*River Frome*	Ashford	12/25	Ashford 6/28

Plate 127: No. A890 *River Frome* stands at Bricklayers Arms Shed in December 1925 shortly after its construction at Ashford.
Author's Collection

Plate 128: A Cannon Street to Dover train passes London Bridge headed by No. A890 *River Frome*, shortly after entering traffic.

Lens of Sutton

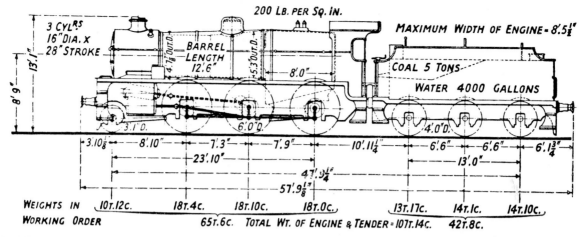

200 LB. PER SQ. IN.

3 CYL^RS 16" DIA. X 28" STROKE

MAXIMUM WIDTH OF ENGINE = 8'.5¼"

BARREL LENGTH 12.6"

COAL 5 TONS

WATER 4000 GALLONS

WEIGHTS IN WORKING ORDER	10T.12C.		18T.4C.	18T.10C.	18T.0C.	13T.17C.	14T.1C.	14T.10C.
		65T.6C.				42T.8C.		

TOTAL WT. OF ENGINE & TENDER = 107T.14C.

HEATING SURFACE, TUBES—					
LARGE AND SMALL	...	...	...	...	1,390·6 SQ. FT.
FIREBOX	...	...	...	...	135·0 ,,
TOTAL (EVAPORATIVE)	...	...	...		1,525·6 ,,
SUPERHEATER	...	...	...	...	285·0 ,,
COMBINED HEATING SURFACES	...	...	...	1,810·6 ,,

SUPERHEATER ELEMENTS	...	...	...	21–1¾ IN. DIA. OUTS.
LARGE TUBES	...	... 21–5¼ IN. DIA. OUTS. ⎫	12 FT. 10⅛ IN.
SMALL TUBES	...	... 173–1¾ IN. DIA. OUTS. ⎬	BET. TUBEPLATES
GRATE AREA	...	...	...	25·0 SQ. FT.
TRACTIVE EFFORT (AT 85 PER CENT. B.P.)	...	25,387·0 LB.

Figure 7: The drawing depicts the class, Nos. A891-A900 and Nos. 1901-1910. No. A890 *River Frome* emerged from Ashford Works in June 1928 as a 2-6-0 tender engine minus its name, but still retaining the Holcroft valve gear to the middle cylinder.

U1 Class

The Holcroft valve gear had proved troublesome, in particular the over running of the inside valve gear due to wear in the various pin joints. Maunsell was impressed by the performance of the 3-cylinder version, in particular for its better acceleration and smoother running, but when the U1 class was built, three sets of Walschaerts valve gear were provided, later converting No. A890 bringing it into line with the rest of the class.

Their duties included many semi-fast passenger and freight workings and speeds of up to 80m.p.h. were recorded with loads of 300 tons, although the official maximum was 70 m.p.h.

In the war years, they were found most useful because of their high route availability, and were in the forefront of troop train operations over the Hastings line.

In BR days, before the Kent Coast electrification, they handled a large amount of main line passenger work on summer Saturdays. In 1954, a trial was made on the Somerset & Dorset line with No. 31906, with a view to replacing the 'Black Fives', but they could not equal the performance of the larger engines.

New cylinders were provided for many of the class from 1954, including No. 31890, and some also received BR blast pipes and liners.

The entire class had 30,000 added to their numbers on nationalisation, except for Nos. 1891 and 1901, which ran for a time with an 'S' prefix. They eventually came into line in May 1948 and November 1949 respectively. Apart from the modifications mentioned, the class remained unaltered throughout their lives and were withdrawn at the end of 1962 in line with the Southern Region policy at that time. The last of the class to be withdrawn was No. 31910 in July 1963. None of the class were preserved.

Summary of the Maunsell 3-Cylinder U1 class Locomotives

Loco. No.	Built	Date Built	Date Withdrawn	Loco. No.	Built	Date Built	Date Withdrawn
A891	Eastleigh	1/31	4/63	1901	Eastleigh	6/31	6/63
A892	Eastleigh	1/31	11/62	1902	Eastleigh	7/31	11/62
A893	Eastleigh	2/31	12/62	1903	Eastleigh	7/31	12/62
A894	Eastleigh	2/31	12/62	1904	Eastleigh	7/31	11/62
A895	Eastleigh	3/31	12/62	1905	Eastleigh	8/31	12/62
A896	Eastleigh	3/31	12/62	1906	Eastleigh	9/31	12/62
A897	Eastleigh	3/31	11/62	1907	Eastleigh	9/31	12/62
A898	Eastleigh	4/31	12/62	1908	Eastleigh	10/31	12/62
A899	Eastleigh	4/31	12/62	1909	Eastleigh	10/31	12/62
A900	Eastleigh	5/31	12/62	1910	Eastleigh	11/31	7/63

Plate 129:   No. A890, as rebuilt as a nameless 2-6-0 Mogul, still retaining the conjugated valve gear and massive steps to the running plate, is pictured at Ewer Street in 1928.

S. C. Nash Collection

Plate 130:   A 'down' mid-morning slow train prepares to stop at Knockholt, headed by No. A890, in July 1928.

Author's Collection

Plate 131: No. 31890, in BR lined black livery, at Eastleigh on 15th July 1951, the conjugated valve gear having been replaced by three sets of Walschaerts valve gear. The massive steps to the footplate have been replaced by steps behind the front buffer beam.

L. Elsey

Plate 132: No. A893, fresh from Eastleigh Works a few weeks before, heads an 'up' Portsmouth to Waterloo express in March 1931 and passes Raynes Park. These trains were scheduled to cover the 79½ miles between Portsmouth Town and Waterloo non-stop in 98 minutes. Smart work was required on the part of the crews if time was to be kept.

Photomatic

Plate 133: An August 1931 view of No. 1905, resplendent in the Southern Railway passenger livery, shortly after construction at Eastleigh, and pictured about to leave London Bridge for the South Coast.

Author's Collection

Plate 134: The summer of 1937 saw a number of J1 locomotives transferred to the West Country to be shedded at Exmouth Junction. The intention was to replace the T9 class 4-4-0s, but it was found the J1 class was rather heavy on coal and water, as well as suffering excessive wear to the leading flanges. By late 1939, they were transferred to Guildford and Redhill to work the heavy wartime traffic. No. 1898 prepares to leave Plymouth (North Road) for Exeter, via Okehampton, in 1938.

Lens of Sutton

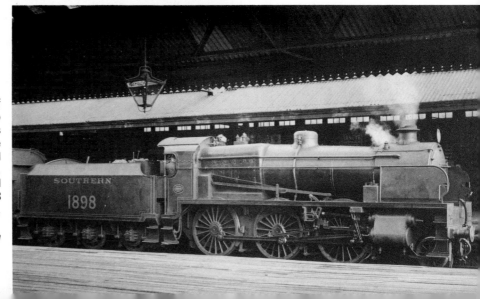

WEST COUNTRY IN THE 1960s

Plate 135: A meat container special, hauled by No. 31899, is bound for Nine Elms from North Devon, having just joined the Western Region main line at Cowley Bridge Junction on 5th July 1961.

R. C. Riley

Plate 136: Holiday-makers see their friends off on an August 1961 morning Padstow to Exeter train which is waiting to leave behind No. 31903.

Author's Collection

Plate 137: No. 31902 leaves Port Isaac Road with a Padstow to Exeter train on 12th July 1961. In June 1961, following the end of steam on the South Eastern Division, several of the class were transferred to Exmouth Junction. Their stay in the west was short, and they were soon sent to the Central Division.

R. C. Riley

Plate 138: Ex-works No. 1896 in plain black with the Bulleid-style 'Southern' on the tender, and cab numerals, photographed at Ashford on 6th July 1946. Around this time, No. 1896 was fitted with a 6in. square duct which was permanently open in the base of the smokebox, and through which ash cinders and char could be dispersed via a chute on to the track. This device performed reasonably well and was incorporated in Bulleid's 'Leader' class design. Exact dates of fitting and removal of this device are not known.

R. C. Riley

Plate 139: In early British Railways plain black livery, with smokebox snifting valves removed, No. 31910 waits to go on shed at Brighton on 11th June 1948.

L. Elsey

Plate 140: A through Hastings to Birkenhead train leaves Redhill on 25th June 1951 with No. 31900 at its head. It is bound for Reading where another locomotive change will take place, handing over to the Western Region.

Brian Morrison

Plate 141: No. 31908 emerges from Somerhill Tunnel, on 19th April 1958, and coasts down the 1 in 103/47 incline to Tonbridge with the 2.45p.m. Tunbridge Wells West to Tonbridge train, formed of an ex-LBSC push-pull set.

R. C. Riley

Plate 142: On 6th August 1958, No. 31984 shuts off for the speed restriction through Lewes with an Army Cadets' special from Brighton to Shorncliffe, Kent.

R. C. Riley

Plate 143: A Victoria to Newhaven Harbour boat train crosses the River Ouse at Southerham Junction on 28th July 1953 headed by No. 31902.

L. Elsey

Plate 144: No. 31906, in full cry, passes Clapham (Eastern) with the 11.50 Victoria to Ramsgate train on 20th April 1957.

S. C. Nash

Plate 145: On 8th August 1959, No. 31894 stalled whilst attempting to get away from a signal check at North Pole Junction on the West London Extension line whilst on a Eastbourne to Birmingham through train. Assistance is being given by rebuilt 'West Country' class locomotive No. 34046 *Braunton* as far as Willesden where both locomotives hand over to a London Midland Region engine. No. 34046 had previously worked another inter-regional train to Willesden, and was awaiting the return working when help was requested.

R. C. Riley

U1s ON THE EASTERN SECTION

Plate 146: The sole rebuilt U1 class locomotive, No. 31890, works a Ramsgate to Victoria train, and is pictured passing St. Mary Cray Junction on 18th May 1959.

R. C. Riley

Plate 147: A Dover to Charing Cross via Faversham train, headed by No. 31900, is seen on the loop line at St. Mary Cray Junction on 14th June 1958.

R. C. Riley

Plate 148: On 8th November 1952, in wintry sunshine, No. 31906 pulls away from a signal check at Chisel-hurst whilst working empty coaching stock from London Bridge to Dover.

Brian Morrison

Plate 149: A rather grimy No. 31893 leaves Cannon Street with the 5.38p.m. commuter train for Dover on 30th May 1958.

R. C. Riley

U1s ON THE WESTERN SECTION

Plate 150: A Waterloo to Bournemouth excursion train, formed of early Southern Railway corridor stock, commonly known as 'Ironclads', leaves Eastleigh on 12th July 1952.

L. Elsey

Plate 151: On the morning of 9th March 1961, No. 31891 gallops down Knowle Bank, near Fareham, with a Lancing to Eastleigh stock train.

L. Elsey

Plate 152: A troop special from Windsor
Southampton Docks, headed by No.
1893, passes Bevois Park Sidings, near St.
enys, on 14th June 1961.

W. M. J. Jackson

Plate 153 (left): No. 31908, is pictured on Eastleigh coaling stage, on
20th April 1961, and waits for the
enginemen to take it on shed for the
next turn of duty.

L. Elsey

Plate 154: Rebuilt U1 class No. 31890
its final form. Pictured at Eastleigh
10th April 1963, it has BR a.w.s.
ted, the yellow triangle on the cab
noting water treatment in use, 25kV
ctrification warning flashes on the
ebox, and smoke deflectors. The
sed running plate over the cylinders
d the 3,500 gallon tender distin-
ishes it from the rest of the class.

L. Elsey

PRESERVED LOCOMOTIVES

Plate 155: On 23rd October 1983, a double-headed special from Alresford climbs to Ropley behind preserved U class locomotive No. 31806 and N class No. 31874 *Brian Fisk*, on the Mid-Hants Railway.

Mick Roberts

Plate 156: Sixteen years after withdrawal from British Railways service, U class locomotive No. 1618, having been restored to running order in Southern Railway passenger livery on the Bluebell Railway, heads the 15.32 Sheffield Park to Horsted Keynes train, near Holywell, on 18th June 1978.

John Scrace

Plate 157: The 18.05 Ropley to Alresford train, on the Mid-Hants Railway, prepares to leave Ropley headed by N class locomotive No. 31874 *Aznar Line* on 16th July 1978. This locomotive was named by a shipping line in April 1977, and carried the name until its removal in January 1979. Later the same year, No. 31874 was renamed *Brian Fisk*, the nameplate being carried on the footplate in a manner similar to the Southern Region Standard Class 5s in BR days.

John Scrace

Plate 158:   A fine sight, as U class No. 31806 emerges from Alresford Cutting with the 12.50 Boxing Day special from Alresford to Medstead and Four Marks on 26th December 1983. This U class locomotive is unusual in having a 4,000 gallon straight-sided tender, normally carried in BR days by the N1 class and a few Maunsell S15 class 4-6-0s. The tender arrived from Barry scrapyard behind another U class, No. 31625, which is undergoing restoration at the present time at Ropley.

Mick Roberts